T0108223

ART LEGENDS ALPHABET

Words by Robin Feiner

Aboriginal and Torres Strait Islander people are advised that this book includes the images and names of people who have passed away.

A is for **A**ndy Warhol. This renegade turned high art on its head, and carved out a place for popular culture in art galleries. His legendary screen prints of iconic images – like Marilyn Monroe and Campbell's soup cans – defined a new genre known as Pop art.

B is for Jean-Michel **B**asquiat. Emerging from New York's punk scene in the 1970s, this graffiti artist brought the grit of the streets to the 80s high art scene. His collage-style paintings with African-Caribbean influences were like the Hip Hop of visual art.

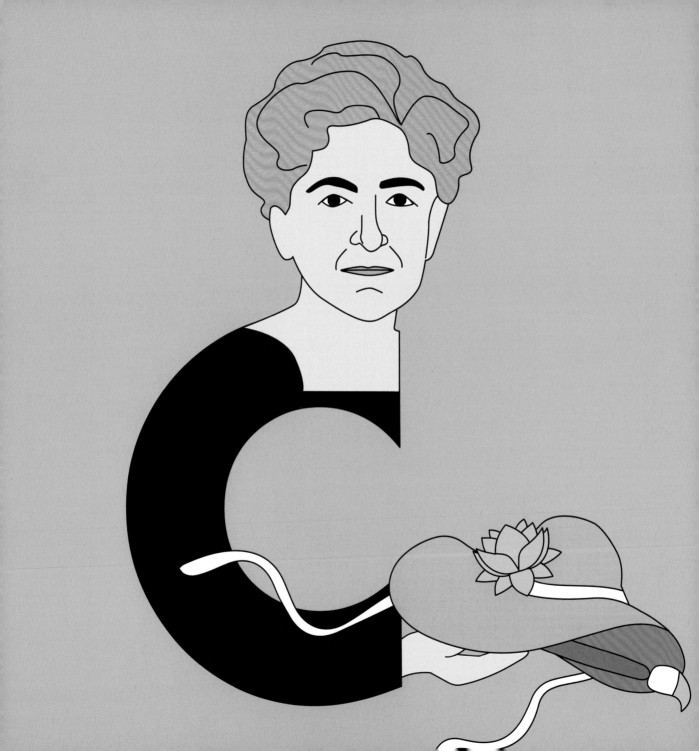

C is for Mary Cassatt. Determined to forge a career as an artist, this American painter moved to France against her father's wishes, and developed her art. Her perseverance paid off, and her Impressionist paintings of women and children became legendary.

D is for Salvador **D**ali. One of the most prolific surrealists of the 20th Century, this boundary-pushing legend was a skilled all-rounder. From clocks melting in the sun to distorted faces suspended in the landscape, his work is like a twisted dream.

E is for Elisabeth Louise Vigée Le Brun. This Parisian painter produced over 600 portraits during her illustrious career. Her signature style presented subjects gracefully and elegantly, and was popular with aristocrats and royalty, including Marie Antoinette and Queen Catherine of Russia.

F is for **F**rida Kahlo. Well-recognized by her floral headpieces and legendary mono-brow, Kahlo's self-portraits depicted her Mexican heritage, as well as her struggles with a physical disability. She inspirationally once said, "Feet, what do I need you for when I have wings to fly?"

G is for Vincent van **G**ogh.
This tortured 19th-century
artist transferred his emotions
onto canvas in thick, layered
brushstrokes. His painting of
a blue midnight sky covered in
swirling yellow stars inspired
the pop song, 'Starry,
Starry Night.'

H is for **H**enri Matisse. Considered the greatest colorist of the 20th Century, Matisse used blocks of pure color as the basis for his bold, expressive paintings. As an impressionist, he wanted his pieces to convey the "light joyousness of springtime."

I is for Robert Indiana. Often confused for a pop artist, this minimalist painter and sculptor transformed everyday objects into eye-catching works of art. His LOVE series, where the letters of the word 'love' are stacked, is so legendary it has been celebrated on a postage stamp.

J is for Jackson Pollock. This trailblazing abstract impressionist didn't so much paint his canvases as hurl and drip and splash color onto them! An American modernist legend, he threw out the rule book and the standard paint brush with it.

K is for Emily **K**ame Kngwarreye. Living in a remote Australian desert town, Emily became an international success at the age of 80! Producing 3,000 paintings in her eight-year professional career, this Indigenous Australian drew inspiration from her strong connection to her heritage.

L is for Roy Lichtenstein. Taking his cues from pop culture graphics and comic strips, Lichtenstein was the first American Pop artist to gain widespread attention. His iconic 'image and word bubble' style paintings were the internet memes of their time.

M is for **M**ichelangelo.
From the mural on the ceiling of the Sistine Chapel to his iconic marble sculpture of 'David,' this legendary master of the Italian Renaissance was a creative genius. His emotive renderings of biblical scenes are still as popular today.

N is for Norman Rockwell. This iconic author, painter and illustrator depicted the 'American Dream' in warm, affectionate images. Featured mainly in the Saturday Evening Post magazine, his colorful representations of American small-town life are truly legendary.

O is for Georgia **O**'Keeffe. From a stylized New York skyline to a beautifully magnified flower, this American modernist worked with simplicity to capture the power of objects, big and small. Her iconic watercolor, 'Blue II,' captures the scroll-shaped neck of the violin she played.

P is for Pablo Picasso.
The most influential artist of
the early 20th Century, this
legend took conventional form
and rearranged it to pioneer
Cubism. His talent moves easily
from the melancholic portraits
of his famous Blue Period to
the furious protest of his war
mural, 'Guernica.'

Q is for Jaune **Q**uick-to-See Smith. Internationally known for her insightful socio-political commentary, this Native American visual artist uses mixed media to layer her canvases with strong messages around human rights, the environment, and her people's history and culture.

Rr

R is for Bridget **R**iley. With her early work inspired by French artist Georges Seurat's pointillist technique of using small dots to create an image, Riley then developed her own Op Art signature style, which uses geometric shapes to create optical illusions.

S is for Cindy **S**herman. Born into the 'Pictures Generation' of the mid-20th Century, this legend sought to use photography, not as a mirror to society, but as a critical reflection. Her iconic and carefully curated 'snapshots' explore the effects of mass media on modern life.

T is for **T**racey Emin. Often referred to as the 'bad girl of British art,' this conceptual artist uses her own emotional history – and often her own body – to create drawings, videos and installations that explore her personal demons.

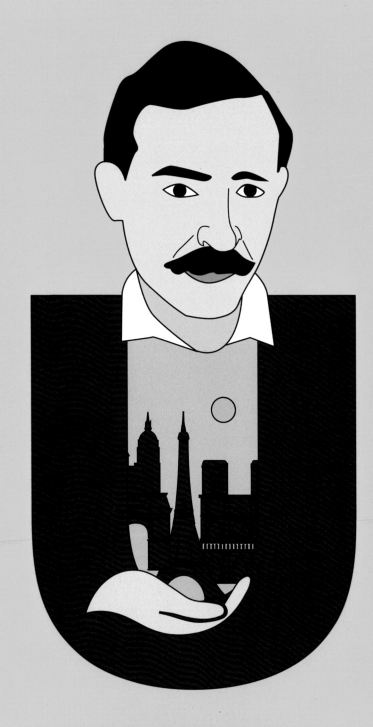

U is for Maurice **U**trillo.
This French bohemian painter
was one of the pioneers of
'The School of Paris,' an
experimental group of artists
formed post-World War I.
Utrillo's iconic paintings of
Parisian street scenes are
still mimicked by street
artists today.

V is for Leonardo da **V**inci. Anatomist, inventor, writer, painter and sculptor, da Vinci was the original Renaissance Man! He changed the way we see the human body with his 'Vitruvian Man' sketch, and his 'Mona Lisa' still intrigues with her enigmatic smile.

W is for **W**assily Kandinsky. This legend of abstract modern art inspired generations of young artists with his ability to express emotion through color and form. His vibrant compositions explode across the canvas like a fierce piece of music.

X **is for Alexander Calder. This 20th-century artist redefined sculpture by making his suspended pieces move through space using motorized elements and floating 'mobile' forms. His monumental sculptures have transformed public spaces in major cities all over the world.**

Y is for **Y**ayoi Kusama. Using her mental illness as inspiration for her paintings, sculptures, installations and photography, this legendary conceptual artist has become one of the most unique and famous contemporary artists of her time.

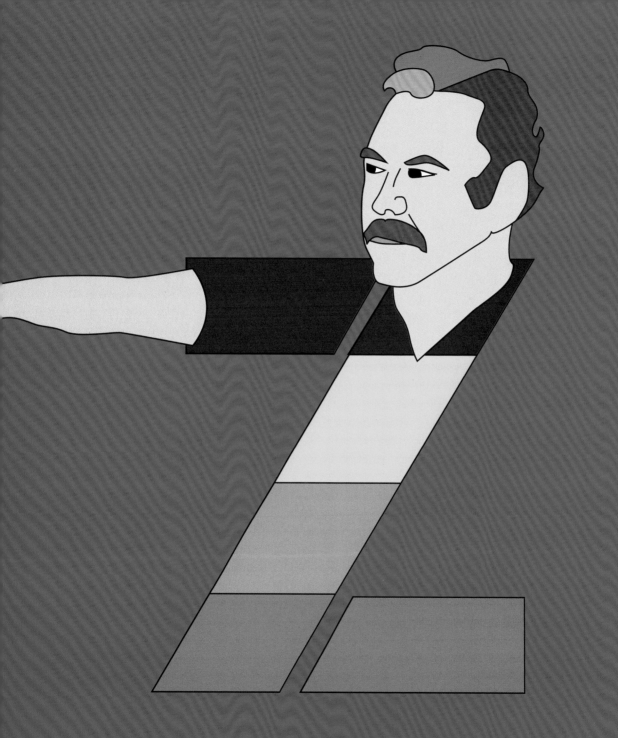

Zz

Z is for Larry **Z**ox. Working in painting and printmaking, this abstract expressionist created graphic artworks that balanced color and form perfectly. From flat geometric blocks to broad brushstrokes of color, his work is lyrical and bold all at once.

The ever-expanding legendary library

EXPLORE THESE LEGENDARY ALPHABETS & MORE AT WWW.ALPHABETLEGENDS.COM

ART LEGENDS ALPHABET
www.alphabetlegends.com

Published by Alphabet Legends Pty Ltd in 2019
Created by Beck Feiner
Copyright © Alphabet Legends Pty Ltd 2019

UNICEF AUSTRALIA
A portion of the Net Proceeds from the sale of this book
are donated to UNICEF.

9 780648 506331

The right of Beck Feiner to be identified as the author and
illustrator of this work has been asserted by her in accordance
with the Copyright Amendment (Moral Rights) Act 2000.

This work is copyright. Apart from any use as permitted
under the Copyright Act 1968, no part may be reproduced,
copied, scanned, stored in a retrieval system, recorded or
transmitted, in any form or by any means, without the prior
use of the publisher.

This book is not officially endorsed by the people and
characters depicted.

Printed and bound in China.

ALPHABET LEGENDS